PRAISE FOR ACROSS THE DIFFICULT

"I am grateful for this book. A book of history and bravery, poems that burst through silences of centuries, unafraid of either bliss or agony. Tamam Kahn has become a branch on the mighty tree of knowledge that is women's knowledge of the unbreakable connection between flesh and spirit. She declares, and we all can declare, 'We could have world history rewritten. Right now. Why not?'"

> — Alicia Ostriker, author of *Waiting for the Light* and *The Volcano and After*

"What a joy to read Tamam Kahn's *Across The Difficult*! Some approach the Sufi tradition like a fossil, an icon of a bygone era, or an artifact we encounter in a museum. Tamam's beautiful book is a reminder that the Sufi tradition is a living tradition, a river of transmission, that has come from the Divine Beloved and will sweep us up to carry us back Home. What a lovely echo of Rabi'a, the giant beacon of love in the Islamic tradition, is Tamam's intimate book. Highly recommended for all spiritual seekers, and those who have been touched by the Sufi tradition."

> — Omid Safi, professor of Asian and Middle Eastern Studies at Duke University, and founder of *Illuminated Courses and Tours*

"Tamam Kahn has offered us a treasure in her new book, *Across the Difficult*. Across worlds, through her words, one feels the presence of the dear ones, the women of heart and deep soul who have come before us; among whom Tamam now stands. May her words encourage and support many souls in their journeying, as they, likewise, come to meet themselves: 'shining right through the difficult.'"

> — Camille Adams Helminski, author of *Women of Sufism* and *The Way of Mary: Maryam Beloved of God*

"Ms. Kahn's masterful work evidences the mystery of a communing with blessings that is unimpeded by space, time, culture, and yes, even death itself. These poems come from and remind us of the eternal flow of grace that reaches our hearts with meanings, love, and wonder."

> — Jonathan Granoff, president of the
> Global Security Institute

"Our hurting world is calling for women's wisdom. In this new collection, thanks to Tamam Kahn's rich imagination, vital intuition, and vivid imagery, readers can become intimate with and inspired by one of Islam's most important women mystics and others whose vitality and insight might otherwise have been lost."

> — Krista Bremer, collaborator,
> storyteller, author of *A Tender Struggle*

ACROSS THE DIFFICULT

WITH RABIA OF BASRA AND OTHERS

POEMS BY

Tamam Kahn

Albion
Andalus
Boulder, Colorado
2023

*"The old shall be renewed,
and the new shall be made holy."*
— Rabbi Avraham Yitzhak Kook

Albion-Andalus Inc.
P. O. Box 19852
Boulder, CO 80308
www.albionandalus.com

Design and composition by Albion-Andalus Books

Cover design by Hauke Sturm

Cover photo by Yevhen Andruschenko

ISBN-13: 978-1-953220-26-4 (Paperback)

ISBN-13: 978-1-953220-27-1 (Hardcover)

Manufactured in the United States of America

And making sure to live—
to go through life not around it—
is always hard.

— Jorie Graham, Poet

Over a decade ago, I purchased *The Book of Seventy* by poet Alicia Ostriker. She signed it, "For Tamam and the quest for difficult truth." She had written a beautiful blurb in my first book, which she called, "a bridge between worlds."

This book is dedicated to
Alicia Ostriker

CONTENTS

FOREMOTHERS ACROSS HISTORY

DIFFICULT TRUTH

ACKNOWLEDGEMENTS

Gratitude & thanks for wisdom and support from:

Wendy Taylor Carlisle, Ghulam Rasool Dehlvi, David Daud Peck, Netanel Miles-Yépez, Daniel Jami, Hauke Jelaluddin Sturm, Ammon Haggerty, Ayat Kindschi, Pir Shabda Kahn, the Sufis of Morocco and Syria, and to the memory of scholar and my good friend, Arthur Buehler.

PREFACE

What was it like to write this book of poetry? Emily Dickenson expresses my early knowledge of the process:

> I stepped from plank to plank
> A slow and cautious way
> The Stars about my Head I felt
> About my Feet the Sea.
>
> I knew not but the next
> Would be my final inch—
> This gave me that precarious Gait
> Some call Experience. (#875)

We are all crossing the sea of life, experiencing wild and calm currents while held in its flow. Words may lift us above the water. This rope bridge, held by historic mentioning across centuries, could be missing an occasional wooden plank. We move through stories, spread out, and then, condensed and star-packed, we are squeezed into the birdhouse of poetry to be hatched and sung, filling the air with music—beyond the difficult.

Ah, yes! *metaphor*, is called by esteemed British poet Ruth Padel "one of the big natural adventures of all language." She quotes Sir Jonathan Miller who writes: "Finding out what something is—is largely a matter of discovering what it is like."[1] I become curious, fresh-hearted, and softened. Here I am! Ready to move into the realm of women's history.

The first section of this book is 'Rabia Al-Adawiyya of Basra.' Yesterday's stories of famous and brave women begin here with Rabia—a great Sufi Mystic from the 8th century, whose path leads through the *Unity of Being*. This word *Sufi* means to me *fragrance across blooming flowers of religion*. I breathe in, then share Rabia's multiple gifts.

Part two addresses *Foremothers Across History*. For more than a decade I traveled to some of Morocco's most vibrant locales—Fez, Marrakesh, Oujda—where I met local women gathering several times weekly to sing and chant, in accord with very old Islamic Sufi traditions. They drew me into their homes and covered my hands with henna tattoos. All around us was the scent of divine flowers. In 1999, I joined several thousand women at the *Eid al-Mawlid* (Celebration of the Prophet's birthday), and their collective, joyful strength amazed me.

These experiences ultimately led to decades of researching and writing poetry on the women of early Islam. I spent time in India and Syria, uncovering threads of old stories and weaving them into a fresh perspective. In Fez, Morocco, twenty years ago I prayed in the mosque at the ancient university, the Qarawiyyin. Today women's movements may be restricted there.

I felt the blessings of the Prophet Muhammad's grand-daughter Sayyida Zaynab and her niece Ruqayya. I visited their celebrated burial centers in and near the city of Damascus, Syria. Reaching back to the mythical past, I explored such figures as Eve, (known as *Grandmother Eve* in Arabia) and Hagar, mother of Ishmael. The poems I wrote invoke these enduring female figures and tell of their great hardship.

Last is part three: *Difficult Truth*. All over the world today the media speaks of war, starvation, and capture. Families are desperate to leave dangerous places. Women in Afghanistan are unable to experience higher education. May we—who are free to read these poetic stories—honor those who struggle, and may we aspire to see them free from dark difficulty, now and in the future.

xiv

Wherever you may be, I invite you to join me crossing the difficult, in the footsteps of the blessed women—and men—remembered here.

RABIA AL-'ADAWIYYA OF BASRA

THE WOMAN WHO NEVER DIES

INTRODUCTION

Rabia al-Adawiyya was unique because in her relations with God and her knowledge of things divine she had no equal; she was highly respected by all the great mystics of her time and she was a decisive proof, an unquestioned authority, to her contemporaries.[1]

Sufi Farid al-Din al-'Attar (13th century) helped bring together the stories of Rabia's myth from which the narrative of her life and activities unfolded.[2] It is said that her stories are legendary rather than factual. Was she an actual historical person? Over time she emerged from mythical oral traditions.

She was said to have lived in the 8th century in Basra, in Southern Iraq, close to the Persian Gulf. Since most freewomen in Islam at that time were under the guardianship of a father, uncle, or brother, it is written that she spent time alone in slavery. She is known, not as "the daughter of—" but is called by her tribe's name, *al-Adawiyya*. Some list her as a *hurra*, (a free woman) probably from an Arab tribe.

It is told that she was orphaned as a young girl and became a slave. She would pray for Union with God, sometimes going without sleep to continue her all-night vigils. One evening her master saw a blinding light above her head as she prayed. He was shocked and set her free. She traveled into the wilderness and became intimately connected to God, entering and reaching mystical mastery. No duality, only Love-Unity for all.

3

Attar writes in *Conference of the Birds* Rabia's prayer: "O God, you who know the secret of all things, bring to pass the worldly desires of my enemies, and grant my friends the eternity of future life. But as for me, I am free of both . . . I need only You. If I should turn my eyes toward the two worlds, or desire anything but You, I should be no more than an unbeliever."[3]

Rabia taught honesty and Love of God in the form of aphorisms, wisdom teachings and her own asceticism. She showed that devotion to God may be transformed to love of God. She was a bringer of the Mystical path to Islamic teaching. "A mystic is one who meets the everydayness of life as an opportunity not only to become whole herself, but to bring the elixir of love to the broken world."[4] She is greatly valued within the many countries and divisions of Islam today.

Tales of Rabia often show her as divine and saintly. The poems in this book aim to bring her into focus as a timeless, living woman we might converse with. She is a feminine light, a clear-headed teacher, unexcelled and accredited by nearly all the great men of her time and later.

She comes to life in her poetic lines, and *insh'Allah*—in the following poems as well.

4

Selected Quotes of Rabia

"You know of the how, but I know of the how-less."

"Death is a bridge between friends.
The time now nears that I cross that bridge,
and friend meets Friend."

"Allah: The Stars are shining,
and the eyes of man are closed
and kings have shut their doors,
and every lover is alone with his beloved,
and here am I alone with Thee."

"I swear that ever since the first day
You brought me back to life,
The day You became my Friend,
I have not slept—
And even if You drive me from your door,
I swear again that we will never be separated—
Because You are alive in my heart."

"Marriage has to do with being—
But where can this be found?
I should belong to you?
What makes you think
I even belong to myself?
I am His—His!"

"In my soul
there is a temple,
a shrine, a mosque, a church
that dissolves,
that dissolves in God"

"I grieve not because I am sorrowful;
I am grieved at my own lack of sorrow."

5

Here

Here I am.   Rabia-of-Basra.
You recognize me—rough clothes
and a hut you couldn't sleep in.

Don't look to me for sappy love clichés.
Moral righteousness.
Holy ambition.
Feel good promises.

Don't look at me with those hungry eyes.
I severed my heart
from trickery,
from lies and self-praise,
from sweet seduction
and doubletalk.

I taste awakening.
Hear galaxies,
feel God-in-Everything.

I am here.
Revised.
Improvised and self-realized.
Revolutionized.

They say I am Doorkeeper of the Heart.
The Woman Who Never Dies.

Love's Prize.

EPISTOLARY POEM

Dear Rabia,
I'm writing you to clarify the meaning
of this now famous quote:

> *I carry a torch in one hand*
> *and a jug of water in the other . . .*
> *I am going to set fire to heaven*
> *and I'll snuff the flames of hell.* [1]

A knot of fire on a stick . . .
you run with it through the heavenly streets,
shoes burning—
while you pour from *the jug*,
sloshing down the grate of hell
a deluge that drowns flame after flame.

I struggle with this torrent. To me it's airlessness,
engulfed in fire and water
gasping for happiness no matter what.
Our planet burns with us on it.

Torch and Jug. Torch and Jug.

I am cracked open.
Inhaled, cooled and perfect
finding *Breath* within the breath.
Completely here.
Is that what you want us to know?
That I can stop choosing heaven or hell.

I look forward to your reply.
With you in Unity,

Tamam Kahn

TREE STORY

But even the great Rabia of Basra is not included
in any lineage genealogy. Where are the women?
The answer is uncomfortably obvious—silent
and silenced by patriarchal culture, buried
in the footnotes of history.

> Netanel Miles-Yépez,
> *In the Teahouse of Experience*

The tree is bearing centuries of mystics,
each name engraved on branch or trunk.
Ancestry's lineage without women.
All female names tumble off the bark, lost
in bird blur—patriarchy's murmurations.
Women! Now is the time to howl strong as
a hundred elephants. To cry: *FOUL!*
We can push on the trunk, demand a change.
Rabia al-'Adawiyya—you must be seen
on the tree of genealogy. We lift
your name and that of other mighty Mothers—
up the bark, the trunk, and down through roots.
We're in this tree dance. Let old thinking die.
Matriarchy buds and bloomifies.

8

RÉSUMÉ

Woman
flows famously from man's rib
    held together with knowing
    like the fluid strength of the jellyfish
    in Adam's Ocean

Woman
goes a-slide with the tide trailing tentacles
    onto the continent holding life to come
    there on her own two legs and feet

She
strides alive with predestination
    toe to crown right into self-monarchy

Rabia
is *the crown of men—although a woman* [1]
a *murshida* [2] the queen of mystical teaching

Woman
    Out from the rib bone
        Under among jellyfish
            Above solid ground
                Inside the crown

Rabia
carries love's keys to the unknowable

BEYOND PILGRIMAGE

Any second the soul can stand up
and start across the desert, as does Rabia.

Robert Bly[1]

Can I make sense of this story they tell me?
Nine-hundred miles between Basra and Mecca!

Rabia, walking and walking and walking;
wanting to, trying to, longing for Mecca.

Seems that my word-rhythm moves like the camel
that bears her luggage—no that was a donkey.

Something like thirty-five well stops for camels
Names like: Tha'labiyya, Zurud and 'Afif.

Coated with sand from each pray-bend-and-stretch step:
. . . *seven years prone on her belly she slides to* . . .[2]

Who could do that? "on her belly"—that's crazy.
"Glory of Sacrifice" makes a good story.

Thousands of pilgrims they press toward the Ka'ba.
After those long desert miles circle round it.

Traveler Ebrahim's finally at Mecca,
massive and powerful heart of religion.

Ebrahim looks but the Ka'ba has gone,
the holiest shrine went out to meet Rabia.[3]

10

Both Worlds

Rabia, where do you come from?
From that world.
And where are you going?
To that world.
In this world I am sorrowing.
Eating the bread of this world
and doing the work of that world. [1]

From	This moment the Bread Lounge door is flung open. Bake-and-Take
and where?	as if I've run out of that oven, pushed out
that world is	my inside delight The food of prayer-all-the-time
In this...	My pilot light dims down this sad staircase,
...this world	flavorless. Unable to savor any taste of joy
Sorrowing	as if I were grinding flour in Misery's Bakery
Eating the bread	that smell and taste of a fresh loaf, buttered
work of that world	Hope's slices and crumbs reminding me, Pure Bread's found—everywhere
this, that world	As if my art is tasting *Chureck* [2] sweet bread in both worlds

11

THE POINT OF NEEDLEPOINT

Rabia once taught us: *Like a needle*
be always engaged in the spiritual work.

A house of my childhood
smells of lavender and old leather books.

The tall Victorian archway opens to
the room where two women are talking.

I wait on a bench in the hall.

My grandmother, Elisabeth,
speaks quietly with Rabia of Basra.

Rabia calls me in.

I kiss my grandmother,
then sit in the armchair between
the two women, both alive again.

Rabia smiles. Her hair is wrapped in
woven cloth. Her fingers glide
across a string of wooden beads.

My Grandmother is working, as she does,
with French yarns
and the point of the needle. Each stitch
perfects the pattern in the fabric.

She glances over her glasses at each of us,
and back to her hand-work.
The nine-foot window behind her chair
illuminates the room.

Rabia gestures toward her:

"What an honor to meet Elisabeth,
your grandmother,
a woman who serves a single calling:
great needlepoint artist
in heavenly yarns,
sewing those stories together."

"Learn from her!"

NOTE PASSED TO RABIA

Just this morning I discovered
hidden in a landscape of words
your gifts of bravey—*shajaea* شَجاعة
I heard your whisper:

save the brave words, save bravery
from leaving the frightened world.

Trust me now, Rabia
to keep it going,
to raise the rough weight of it
here in this world

with all that I am.

CREATURES OF THE GAZE

Someone is looking at Rabia.

Someone is lookng at these women:
Marilyn Monroe & Princess Diana
& Mother Theresa & Whitney Houston,
at how they look in in their coffins
in their pretty clothes.   Motionless. Final.

Someone is looking at Rabia,
about to be buried in haste
in her off-white jubbah and scratchy cape
in a simple wooden box, still at last.

Someone is looking at Marilyn Monroe.
She lies in her polished casket
wearing green silk under white tulle.
We can't ask Marilyn: *What happened?*

Two million people watch the procession
bearing Princess Diana in a closed coffin.
She is sheathed in a black, long-sleeved
designer funeral dress.

Mother Theresa rests in an open sarcophagus
clothed in her white nun's robes
with those blue stripes, a cross in her hands.
What happened? They say: . . . *a heart attack.*

We know what happened to Whitney Huston,
in her white lined coffin,
wearing a purple dress and gold slippers.
Death by drugs in her bathtub.

Someone is dreaming they see Rabia,
floating, clothed in green silk edged with gold

and silver. She was buried—as requested—
in her old garments.
What happened to those clothes?

Rabia answers—as if she were suddenly alive—
My finery was folded and sealed until
I was held in the Everlasting Gaze of God.[1]

AFTER SADDAM DRAINED THE WETLANDS OF IRAQ

homeland scarred
with cluster bombs and napalm—
we marsh Arabs,
shredded like a Baghdad newspaper,
are stripped of families, towns
and the breath of our own wetlands.

Basrah (overwatcher)[1] بصره
Legendary Rabia, Mother Nature,
The Woman Who Never Dies
Hear me: you watch over Basra, over
the Tigris and Euphrates plain,
south through date palms, cattails—
water voices, muddy with music.

War years
crippled us. I see thick smog,
beheaded palms, their trunks
like matchsticks burnt in hot wind.
Foreign soldiers climbed
our Sacred Tree of Knowledge,
laughing as the ancient trunk
splits under their weight.

Calling Rabia.
O, Mother Nature, Typhoid and Cholera
slide through the Unfertile Crescent
down river to the sea. Poison and oil.
No call to prayer today. This world is lost!
Did the muezzin just die?

Overwatcher,
watching over Basra. You—
begged for, cried to by the sick,
homeless, and we river-raised children

17

who left this place—
Speak to us, we, the hopeless slaves
of this insanity!

Rabia answers:
When does a slave become contented?
When she is as grateful for adversity
as she is for generosity, abundance for all.[2]

VEIL THEFT

May God steal from you all
                    that steals you from him.
                    Rabia[1]

One night when Rabia is sleeping . . .
several nothings arrive in her small house
all nip and tuck, looking to steal.

One of them sneaks into Rabia's room
and steals her veil.
When the thief tries to leave,
she can't find the door . . .
Finally, she lays the veil aside
and immediately the door opens.

Door disappears. Drop that veil!
Door reappears. *This happens seven times.*

Rabia is still asleep.

From the room a voice speaks:

   "Remember This! Not even Satan
   has enough nerve to try take that veil!
   When one friend is asleep
   the Other is awake and keeping watch." [2]

The thief, released of room theft, walks out
openhanded.

Centuries later a poet tells us:

   "I take with me the emptiness
   of my hands. What you do not have
   you find everywhere."[3]

19

KISĀʿ كساء (CLOTHING)

Rabia, what clothing are you are wearing as
you walk by the water's edge? A full-sleeved
jubbah, coarse cotton not dirty, but colorless.
Woven to last. A gauzy veil that was scrubbed
in well water yesterday, wraps your hair, your
sandals muddied by the Shatt al-Arab River.
Historic scribes leave you clothed in nothing
but words. Holy praise . . . You are *from foot to
face immersed in the Truth . . . robed in the
quintessence of pain . . .* Attar writes.[1] *Robed in*
pain? I watch the fabric move as you walk, spill
and haul water and laugh with the children.
The sun sets, then I see you drape your *kisāʿ* on
a hook by the bed and, from twelve-hundred
years away, I like the practical side of you, as
you slip lightly into a patched nightgown and
sit in the candlelight whispering prayer. Your
old cat purrs in your lap.

TWO TO ONE

Rabia says to God:

I love You with two loves

    Good things come in pairs:

        double scoop   binoculars
        twins   wings
        chopsticks   skis
        socks   shoes
        breasts   headlights

1. A selfish love of passion

      just for me
      jealousy
      lust and distrust
      hidden need and greed
      desire without end

2. And a love that is worthy of You
   God-Love, a love through which
    I see God in everything

      bright flood of LOVE
      constant remembrance
      complete devotion and joy
      mahabba محبة — (mystical love)

All praise is yours for this one and the other.[1]

      Skip further discussion.
      No matter what
      God is love.

RABIA'S MAID TELLS US

the life of Rabia is a thousand apples
plucked with permission
from Heaven's Tree.

DEATH'S PRIZE

Death's heartless angel
snarls a thunderclap
and lowers the black sky with the words:

—I AM THE MURDERER OF JOY,
—THE WIDOWER OF WIVES &
—ORPHAN-ER OF CHILDREN...[1]

Rabia pulls the darkness back
and comforts us, saying:

Angel of Death, listen. Forget the taunt.
Say instead what everyone needs to know:

*—*ALLAH IS YOUR FRIEND.
—YOURS FOREVER—

Death's prize
is bringing friend and Friend together. [2]

23

THE GIFT

You—The Woman Who Never Dies
    all cracked and brittle

You—Rabia, have a grave dug
    in the floor of your home
    shoveled out, dark and empty

You—remember—*tomorrow you'll be here* [1]

You—eyes shut,
    body held still to welcome death

You—right now I see you
    standing on the edge,
    feet bare, clothed in prayer

You—call my name and say to me:

    Touch my hand

        I reach . . . then wake

My fingers
are blooming—*muzhirah* مُزْهِرَة

BLOOMING with poetry

FOREMOTHERS ACROSS HISTORY

"Be what you are.
Give what is yours to give.
Have style. Dare."

— Stanley Kunitz

EVE

After chagrin and apology, Eve—
soon to be Mother-of-All
wraps herself in the cloth of remorse
torn from all heavenly music,
stares at earth's bright darkness,
readies herself for babies,
bullshit and brouhaha.

She asks her children to whisper
how the leaves of paradise
were still imprinted on her hands,
shine of juice on her chin when,
as the Arabs tell: *God forgave her.*

—did you hear that?

This is the story of this forgiveness,
of *Hawwa,* Mother-of-All,
whose name heals us like salve.

PLATE DEPICTING ADAM AND EVE

She is leading, toes near the edge,
about to step out of the dinner plate.
They are both red haired and naked
with Lake Como, a tower and clouds
behind them.

Imagine Restaurante La Punta
long ago serving dinner.
Ravioli al prezzemolo spread across
the image of Adam and Eve,
all covered with pasta
as they move over the green grass.

He glances down at her. Her face
is turned toward his shoulder,
her visible eye seems swollen shut,
her head oddly angled,
back hunched and awkward—
from the fall?

Unforgiveness. This is the story
of how it was and how it will be.
Exposed.

The beginning of blame.

HAGAR

Sarah acted harshly toward Hagar
to the point that Hagar
fled into the wilderness . . .

Genesis 21:9-14

(or was it this . . .)
A woman doesn't start a nation
with a baby and a mule.
Sarah schemed with me,
to make up her jealousy
and push me out
like I pushed Ishmael.
I knew before my baby came—
felt the tearing pain,
saw the well, foresaw
the bright black stone.

He had to take us there,
Far south of Beersheba,
to the wild absence.
He couldn't look at me.
His face was closed.
He simply rode away,
back to his life with Sarah.

I ran between the hills,
as I ran in vision
given me by God.
O, I was mad with thirst
for all I'd left behind.

After Baby Ishmael unearthed
the well of Zamzam with his heel,
after the caravans found us,
after Mecca burst awake around us,
after Abraham returned

28

to build the Ka'ba
here on this land of
water, sun and sand

it's clear my work is done.

SAY IT. TELL US, HAGAR

I can't keep myself from leaving home
following handprints of Divine Being.
My sight opens wider, touched with
love as I'm invited, handed into
an unborn world, its history to come.
I whisper: *God O, God!* crossing deserts.
I'm left here alone with little Ishmael.
My child's eyes stare toward heaven.

A kick—his heel in the sand, then
a drop of water and another, becoming
a fresh spring: *Bi'ru Zamzam* بئر زمزم
Nearby hills and creatures come to drink.
I see footprints of light everywhere,
brilliance along the edges of everything.

NURSE'S DAY

The birthday of Sayyida Zaynab, granddaughter
of Prophet Muhammad is known in Syria
and Iran as "Nurse's Day." (February 25)

Can't keep my hands to myself, I want to grab
the belt fit with explosives, crush & break
the lit-up timer under my heel, then shake
that 17 year old ISIS girl. She has
her dream of paradise. I slap her hard:
Wake up you fool. No, this is not Islam.
They've told you lies. You're just a firebomb
There are no chosen ones and no reward.
This district's hit a second time, consumed
with fear and loss. Close to the holy shrine,
six bombs explode, symbolically malign
you, *Great Sayyida Zaynab* and your tomb.

Wise daughter's daughter of the Prophet, clar-
ify your life, your dignity. Aware,

You challenged tyrant Yazid. Couldn't save
murdered Husayn, the hurricane of pain.
You spoke the truth to power. Here again
we need your voice, a miracle, shockwave.
Can't keep my hands to myself, Want to press
the cheek of a girl a bomb has hurt. Concrete
and bricks, mixed with car-parts on the street.
She's lying here, hijab and flowered dress
soiled in blood, skin struck with cell-phone bits.
Oh Zaynab, legendary nurse— please hand
me lidocaine, a hypodermic and
some tweezers, sterile bandages. Dust is thick.

Assad's war's beyond sane narrative.
We don't know how to stop it. Help us live.

31

CHILD RUQAYYA'S HEXACHORD

You're held inside this story. It repeats,
child witness of the snipped-off lives,
malicious massacre at Karbala. Ruqayya.
Brandished swords in flesh slice life
from life to death that day. You are
a girl of four or six or maybe ten years old.
Hussain, your father, is beheaded here.
The tragedy repeats your name, Ruqayya.
Ruqayya—held with women in a howdah,
held and stowed there like an un-lidded eye,
across dry deserts for five-hundred miles
to the grim palace of Yazid-the-Cruel.
You ask—*where is my father?* He replies:
Here he is. This is his head. Look at it.

Here he is. This is his head. Look at it.
Famished children do not cry, gut squeezed
from war's starvation. See your father's face.
Yazid sees you scream without a voice.
You slip under the weight of unwept tears.
Little girl, once papa lifted you like music,
drew you on his chest for sleep, so safe,
hush now, sweet darling—my habiba.
You're thrown in a cell, peephole for light.
That night, the moon's a fingernail, it's edge
cratered with torn bites, sleepless as the stars,
the stars in open skies. Your fate is clear,
they'll never let you go. Devil Yazid's spell—
You kiss your father. Do you swoon and die?

You kiss your father. Do you swoon and die
or hold your breath in fear? Death closes in
collapsing rescue dreams, release and hope.
Morbid messy memories arrive, repeat.
Just days ago, you feel your earlobes rip when

32

Shim'r, Yazid's soldier grabs your earrings,
Hussain's golden gift. Same day an arrow
pierces baby brother's throat. You look
but see—no rider—father's horse. You know.
You kneel and hug the headless man.
Blood-reddened carnage smears your hands,
face and chest. They catch and tie your
running feet, your hands with rope, again
life tightens, twists—twisting life from inside.

Life tightens, twists—twisting life from inside.
You stand before the throne holding Yazid.
A man asks: *may I have this girl, Ruqayya?*
Sayyida Zaynab, Husain's daughter, glares at
Yazid, commands the room, shouts—*Death*
to Prophet's kin brings your undoing! Her
tongue, becomes a dragon of word-light as
war-room men grow smaller, fade.
Repeated there and in the women's cell
she tells that bleeding narrative of loss.
That haunting night, some say, your father
calls. For you, for him—at last you die.
The floor's your burial. The women cry:
great-granddaughter of God's Prophet—dead!

Great-granddaughter of God's Prophet—dead!
Centuries pass. Thirst from Karbala remains.
Your grave's groundwater spreads. *Stop*
this leaking water now! Young daughter
of the tomb-keeper sees you in vision, dead
and floating; hears you calling out. Your coffin
is exhumed, all soaked in water, packed in mud.
You're there—still young, unharmed, and clean.
Their eyes look on your face. A legend's born,
your story wrapped around you. Dry.
Today you lie enshrined in perfumed silk
inside your casket's shell. With no

immunity against enormity,
here's an eyehole for the world to see you.

Here's an eyehole for the world to see you,
your green tomb in Damascus. I glance up.
A thousand mirrors brighten from above.
Roof-top—*ra'uf,* covers you, Ruqayya. Allah!
Ya Ra'uf means *love through deepest wounds.*
All battered ones who gather, pray for help.
You listen for their grief. They know you know,
have blessings for their pain & sickening fright.
Blue lines in Arabic glow and decorate a wall:
Qur'an 2:201: *O Sustainer, give us goodness,*
virtue in the world and the hereafter.
From all suffering keep us safe!
Ruqayya, Queen of Endlessness,
you're held inside this story. It repeats.

THE QUEEN'S DREAM

A shop window in the Damascus souk
displays the long nightgown
inscribed with the word *hulm* حلم
(Arabic for "a dream.")[1]
I slip into bed that night in the dream-gown.

They say in Ramadan:

Blessing and knowledge of a dream most true
will be given. All difficulties are suspended . . .

I—*The Queen-of-In-Between*—find myself
inside long ago and now, sewn together.

I float through the Al-Assad National Library,
circle the head-shrine of John-the-Baptist,
and pass near the stone room
of Paul-the-Apostle.

I never trust a tyrant,
yet I am here in my nightdress
in the grand hall
of Bashar Assad's Palace Fortress.

       Syria's President stands here
as I move closer until I gaze up into his face.
I remind him:

    All difficulties are suspended!
      Let your people be.

He scowls and gestures to a guard
holding a Glock handgun.
The jewels on my crown sparkle. I don't react.

There is no need to introduce me,

The Queen-of-In-Between.

I tell him:

We could have world history rewritten.
            Right now. Why not?

I wake from the dream and say a prayer
for daring, diplomacy, freedom and the saying:

Blessing and knowledge
                of a dream most true will be given . . .

Outside my window the full moon
hangs her light
as if suspended from a dark branch

            the first night of spring.

NOTES FOR A NARRATIVE

Here is my research for the Qarawiyyin:

Footnote[1] A woman emigré manifested
a famous university, completed in 859 AD.
[1]. . . /al-qarawiyyin-worlds-oldest-university/

**University of al-Qarawiyyin or al-Quaraouiyine
is a university located in Fez, Morocco.
It is the oldest**

> <> MANUSCRIPTS
> Here are four-thousand texts . . . among
> them:
>
> 1. The famous book, *(al-Muwatta')*
> *The Path* written on gazelle sheets

[Hundreds of gazelle-skin pages? Verify this.]

> 2. Kufic Quran pages inscribed on camel
> skin in "square Kufic" They say Kufic was
> inscribed on book pages, textiles, coins...
> ETSY.com/ancient_books

[etsy on-line sign in, search for anything uh oh!
The page you were looking for was not found]

**continually operating as the first degree-
awarding educational institution in the world
according to UNESCO**

[and the Guinness World Records—20 mentions,
but none findable on-line.]

37

<> PHOTOS:
  1. Almohad chandelier made from a giant
     bronze bell won in a battle at Gibraltar
  2. the internal view of the prayer hall
  3. architectural plan
  4. general view
  5. the "timers room" equipped
     with astrolabe, sand clocks, sundials

the oldest (in reference) continual university
([1]www.islamicity.org) **ever and ever.**

  <> INTRODUCTION to detail the following:

  "Al-Qarawiyyin: one of the leading
  spiritual and educational centers
  of the Muslim world was founded
  by a young princess— **Fatima Al-Fihri**
  who migrated from Tunisia to Fez.
  Her determination and finance
  forced construction, then education.

  Great men have taught and learned here,
  prayed here, absorbed wisdom from this
  great center of history."

[What about WOMEN?" ...check on this.][1]

DIFFICULT TRUTH

"I am an abyss that I am trying to cross."

— W.S. Merwin

I'M TELLING YOU

my granddaughters are not held in cages
with blankets of foil.
They eat mac and cheese, sip lemonade
on the porch above the garden.
Their mother brings sweaters and warm pie.

It's a kind of salvation for me that they are ok.
The girls are not hearing explosions,
breathing bomb-dust, not told
to blow themselves up in God's name.

They are not on a raft at sea.
I'm not at sea. My bed is not a raft.
My bed with fluffy pillows is
in a mountain room with
a front door by the driveway.

My belt is not strapped with explosives.
My belt holds eyeglasses,
a pouch with lip gloss, a pen and some cash.
It has two zippers.
I'm telling you the details because I can.

My feet are without dirt, wounds and bruises,
not numb with cold from water's splash.
My darlings do not have to endure
scraps for shoes. They are not pulled away
from their mother and shipped somewhere
behind a wire fence—just held there
until they begin to forget

their mother's voice,
and who they were before.

LEAVING KABUL AIRPORT

Fida is my name, Fida Mohammad
  somebody's son,
    someone's husband,
      someone's new dentist in Kabul

on my way to a new life in America.
  I am outside the moving C-7 aircraft,
  pressed against the landing gear,
  above blurry black tires.

Fida means *redemption* [1] فداء
the one who protects what is most precious
the act of freeing from captivity
exchange, sacrifice.

The plane speeds up. It rolls,
  I am mindless. It lifts me
    held by its thundering
      flying in a hurricane
        prayers forgotten——
    landing gear moves up
   The wheels rush toward me
my hands fail. I lose my grip.

A boy reaches out
now we're two shapes on an I-phone
  as we tumble
    from 200 feet
      onto a flat roof
and die.

A single paper in my jacket pocket
    written carefully—

my father's name and phone number.

TAKEN

Afghani girl, the sun of her
life lost in darkness, young girl,
is peeled like an orange at sunset.
A child running out of childhood,
caught and caught—taken
for marriage early.

Afghani Mother, Grandmother,
each may be held in this shadow:
someone puts a chair-leg on her foot,
pressing.

She really needs to wail, but can't speak—
under her burqa.

An *afghan* is no longer a woolen blanket
but a human being living with death.

It's that feeling
of your raised hands in surrender,
up against the wall
shot twice with a nail gun.

MARIUPOL, UKRAINE

(For Yevhen Andruschenko,
book cover photographer)

I wake to large blast
alone—on the tenth floor.

Shattered window glass all over. Cold
rushes in. No water. No heat. No phone.

The explosion shuts out the sun.
Overcoat over my pajamas. Running.

Running from my home in old slippers—
Over. Across. Down the broken stairway,

urgent voices. Shouts and cries.
No one's waiting for anybody.

Alone, outside in smoke and snow
I am holding my keys, where to?

The sidewalk shakes and rumbles.
I fall to the ground and cover my head.

I scratch at the snow for answers.
Icy cold wind is the reply.

Apartment and car keys still in my hand,
clutched in blood,

My ears ring in a phantom world.
I don't remember where I am.

I taste adrenaline. Someone is lifting me.
I'm alive.
What's next?

UNIVERSITY WOMAN

We the Taliban
will make you
go quiet.
We want
an empty blackboard.
We the Taliban
are erasing the rights
of each one
with breasts
and a vagina
and a clitoris.

Each girl-student and
female professor
splashes silenced outrage
into a ruptured world,
zig-zags suspense
back and forth
across her mind,
hides a spaded heart
raw with hiccups.
Each one cracks open
a brain-leak
of stories and poems,
stashed backpacks
of notebooks filled with
foundational work,
knowledge, science—

all soon to be
academic ditch-litter.

Sahara Ghazal

We wrap blue fabric round us
      like Tuareg nomads, then mount
each kneeling saddled beast. We're up.
      I clutch a passport of silence.

Seated high—so high, I rock from side to side,
      hold on and then, release!
My body opens. Legs stretched wide,
      my soul cavorts in silence.

My camel wants to lead. He's young
      and quick. I say his name
And pat his neck until loud snorts
      erupt to thwart the silence.

East of Zagora lies a view of sand
      and sky, the desert hills.
Three men in robes lead us on foot
      with little effort, all in silence.

The camel has two spread-out toes, tough—
      to take the heat of sand
and rock. This one is quiet now,
      transporting me to silence.

We're crossing heaps of loosened scree,
      and stones. A quilted sky,
brown air, high wind; this sudden sandstorm
      exports the silence.

Our camels kneel, each one a wall for us
      crouched under saddle cloth.
And when the stinging storm's complete,
      we mount. Our escort—silence.

TO BE THERE

Something like one hundred thousand beads
rumble down stone steps. A red and gold
racket. Muhammad kneels there,
                    continues praying.

Tipped from a carton, juice seeps on the floor,
flows to the cushion, all cold, slick and sticky.
Buddha sits there, aware and present,
                    uninterrupted.

Cellphones and murderous, frightening news,
losses and leaf blowers keep me distracted
until I meet myself—shining
                    right through the difficult.

NOTES

PREFACE

1. Ruth Padel, *Silent Letters of the Alphabet*, pp. 12, 13

INTRODUCTION, RABIA OF BASRA: THE WOMAN WHO NEVER DIES

1. Margaret Smith, *Muslim Women Mystics*, p. 71 (Attar, op.cit.I, p. 59)

2. Rkia Elaroui Cornell, *Rabia, From Narrative to Myth*, p. 10

3. Farid ud-Din Attar, *Conference of the Birds*, (Prayer of Rabia), p. 93

4. Mirabai Starr

EPISTOLARY POEM

1. Charles Upton, *Doorkeeper of the Heart*, p. 43

RÉSUMÉ

1. Farid ud-Din Attar, *Conference of the Birds*, p. 51

2. *Murshida* – Sufi term for the one who shows the path (feminine tense)

BEYOND PILGRIMAGE

(In classic literary form: dactylic tetrameter)

1. Robert Bly, "Hiding in a Drop of Water,"
My Sentence Was a Thousand Years of Joy, p. 57

2. Javad Nurbakhsh, *Sufi Women*, p. 36: reference to Attar, *The Conference of the Birds*, #41

3. Ibid., pp. 33, 34.

BOTH WORLDS

1. Margaret Smith, *Muslim Women Mystics*, p. 105

2. *Chureck* is a sweetened pastry, wheel shaped, often stuffed with dates, traditional in Iraq.

NOTE PASSED TO RABIA

1. شَجاعة — *Shajaea* (Ar.) (pronounced se-JAH), 'bravery, courage, daring'

CREATURES OF THE GAZE

1. Javad Nurbakhsh, *Sufi Women* p. 58 (Rabia's death)

AFTER SADDAM DRAINED THE WETLANDS OF IRAQ

1. بصره — *Basrah* (Ar.), 'overwatcher.' Also spelled Basra, Rabia's home.

2. Javad Nurbakhsh, *Sufi Women*, p. 51

VEIL THEFT

1. Charles Upton, *Doorkeeper of the Heart*, opening page

2. Margaret Smith, *Muslim Women Mystics*, p. 54 [italics marks a continuous quote]

3. W.S. Merwin is "a poet"

KISA' كساء (CLOTHING)

1. Javad Nurbakhsh, *Sufi Women*, p. 25 (Quote from Farid ud-Din Attar in *Conference of the Birds*)

TWO TO ONE

1. Rabia's poem "Two Loves" is famous: Charles Upton, *Doorkeeper, of the Heart*, p. 23, #6, & Rkia Elaroui Cornell, *Rabia, From Narrative to Myth*, pp. 197-200

Death's Prize

   1. Charles Upton, *Doorkeeper, of the Heart*, p. 45, #53

   2. Rabia's answer: Ibid., p. 45, #53,

The Gift

   1. Javad Nurbakhsh, *Sufi Women*, p. 56, #6
(She had a grave at home for 40 years)

   2. مزهرة — *muzhira* (Ar.), 'blooming'

Plate Depicting Adam and Eve

(plate) Italian, Urbino, mid 16th century displayed in the
Legion of Honor Fine Arts Museum, San Francisco

Hagar

Hagar is *Hajra* in Arabic and Islamic traditions.

Say It. Tell Us, Hagar

بئر زمزم — *Bi'ru Zamzam* (Ar.), 'the Well of Zamzam' (in Mecca,
Arabia, from Hagar and son Ishmael)

Nurse's Day

January 31st, 2016: two suicide bombs and a car bomb
exploded near Syria's Sayyidah Zaynab Mosque in the town
known as Sitt Zaynab (six miles south of Damascus). At least
60 people were killed and another 110 people were wounded
in the explosions. On February 21st, there was more bombing
and death with no accurate reports of the losses near the
shrine of Sayyidah Zaynab.

Child Ruqayya's Hexachord

Ruqayya was a child of history. She had several first names
and no consistent age. The last month of her life unfolded
with anecdotes told in women's circles centuries ago. Her
father, Hussain, is Shia Islam's most important martyr in

all of history, and she was close-by at his death. Sayyidah Zaynab, her aunt, was imprisoned with her. The mystical tale of her watery coffin awarded Ruqayya fame and an exquisite mosque and shrine in Damascus, there today.

THE QUEEN'S DREAM

1. حلم — *hulm* (Ar.), 'a dream'

NOTES FOR A NARRATIVE

1. Qarawiyyin students were male, but it has been said that "facilities were at times provided for interested women to listen to the discourse while accommodated in a special gallery overlooking the scholars' circle." (reference no longer found online)

LEAVING KABUL AIRPORT

1. فداء — *Fida* (Ar.), 'redemption'

Poems Previously Published

The New Verse Newsletter, '23
"University Woman"
Poets Reading The News, '21
"Taken"
Fahmidan Journal Issue 5, Spring '21
"After Saddam" "The Queen's Dream"
Piccioletta Barca Magazine (UK) May 5, '21
"Child Ruqayya's Hexachord"
The Poet Magazine: Poetry For Ukraine
"Mariupol, Ukraine"
The Poet Magazine: On The Road
"Sahara Camel Ghazal"
The Poet Magazine: Faith
"The Well and Baba Farid"
"Faith's Red Suitcase"
The Poet Magazine *Adversity*
"Child Ruqayya's Hexachord"
"After Saddam"
Antiphone Poetry Magazine (UK) Fall, '16
"Nurse's Day"
PCSJ (Poetry Center San Jose) '22, Caesura
"To Be There"
PCSJ (Poetry Center San Jose) '16. Caesura
"Nurse's Day"
Raven Chronicles: '20 Take a Stand, Art Against Hate
"Nurse's Day"
Young Raven's Literary Review, '19
"I'm Telling You"
Marin Poetry Center Anthology '22
"Leaving Kabul Airport"
Marin Poetry Center Anthology, '20
"I'm Telling You"

Tamam Kahn is the author of poetry books on the mothers of early Islam. *Untold, A History of the Wives of Prophet Muhammad* won an International Book Award in 2010, and *Fatima's Touch* was a finalist in 2016. She has traveled to sacred sites in India, Morocco, and Syria researching early Islamic history and continues to write about history's powerful women. Tamam is a 10th generation American, whose roots go back to America's founding fathers and mothers. She is married to Shabda Kahn, the spiritual director (Pir) of the Sufi Ruhaniat International with outreach in more than 50 countries. For more information on Tamam Kahn and her work, visit: completeword.wordpress.com.